THE AMERICAN PRESIDENTS:

George Washington to Abraham Lincoln

J. SAMUEL REEVES

THE AMERICAN Presidents

GEORGE WASHINGTON

TO

ABRAHAM LINCOLN

Epic Press

Belleville, Ontario, Canada

THE AMERICAN PRESIDENTS:
George Washington to Abraham Lincoln

Copyright © 2003, J. Samuel Reeves

National Library of Canada Cataloguing in Publication

Reeves, Joseph Samuel, 1955-
    The American presidents : George Washington to Abraham Lincoln / Joseph
Samuel Reeves.

ISBN 1-55306-530-1

    1. Presidents--United States--Biography. I. Title.

E176.1.R34 2003   973'.09'9   C2003-900333-7

For more information or
to order additional copies, please contact:

J. Samuel Reeves
4514 Sellman Road
Beltsville, Maryland
20705

Epic Press is an imprint of *Essence Publishing*. For more information, contact: 20 Hanna Court, Belleville, Ontario, Canada K8P 5J2. **Phone**: 1-800-238-6376. **Fax**: (613) 962-3055. **E-mail:** publishing@essencegroup.com **Internet**: www.essencegroup.com

*This book is dedicated to
the victims of September 11
and their families.*

Table of Contents

"When I die, I want to be remembered as a person whose commitment to political and military reforms was resolute, and whose challenging attributes influenced the lives of others."

J. Samuel Reeves

Foreword

The American Presidents: George Washington to Abraham Lincoln, written by Joseph Samuel Reeves, points us to the reality of how our important form of democracy has influenced people and cultures around the world. The history of the U.S. is fairly treated in this book by a good man who believes in the American way of life. He enlightens his readers on how and why the nation came into existence. The commitment to freedom by our founding fathers and values that have characterized this great nation are skillfully presented in this book.

Sam Reeves tells the story of America through the American presidents from a balanced point of view. He writes about the commitments of earlier presidents such as George Washington, John Adams and Thomas Jefferson to leading the fight for a Republican form of government. He presents Washington as the selfless leader who is responsible for peaceful transfer of presidential power that makes our nation the envy of the world. The debates between

Adams and Jefferson on the separation of church and state are dealt with from a historical perspective.

Sam Reeves has given this nation one of the greatest gifts by sharing with the reading public the origin and growth of the U.S. He teaches about the expansion of America and how we gradually became involved in international affairs. Racial and economic problems that have affected our nation are also presented in this book. He uses Abraham Lincoln to highlight the racial tension that almost destroyed the union of our nation. The strength of America is respected because of the constitution of the United States and the fact that no individual or group of individuals can live above the constitution.

Sam Reeves is a very fascinating person who continues to write on different subject matters. This book is one of the best accounts of American presidential history. In these difficult times, when America is at war with terrorism, it is delightful to know that a young man, born in Liberia, Africa, has joined the intellectual debate in educating people about our great heritage.

As an American and a veteran, I want to personally thank Sam Reeves for his great service to our nation. This book should be taught in our schools and kept in our homes. Sam Reeves is a great man, a wonderful scholar and an outstanding part of the American dream. I recommend this book, which is the first in a series on the American presidents, to my fellow Americans and all of our friends.

R.L. "Bob" Bogen
Bloomington, Minnesota
September, 2002

Author's Preface

American political life is one of the most interesting and tempting experiences in all of political history. People of different ages and backgrounds have campaigned for the Oval Office. Many have failed, and few have succeeded in making the White House their place of operation. The American presidency is one of the most powerful and influential offices in the world. The President and his family take precedence everywhere in public or private. Jefferson is right because, no matter how plain or ordinary the President and his family are, the presidency automatically deprives them of their privacy and transforms them into an institution.

The presidency is rooted in the American tradition and dream of freedom, peace and openness. It is also a complex institution that is never fully understood by the very people who are elected into it. Living in the White House (the People's House) as President creates a degree of ownership and expectation that both the House and its occupants are subjects of the people. Washington never lived in the White House but advocated such views through his political philosophy of a weak presidency. He believed that a powerful Congress, a strong judicial system, and a weak executive made up the true formula for balanced government. This would create a government for the people, by the people and of the people.

The orderly transfer of presidential power has been a noble strength of American democracy. This peaceful transition in presidential politics continues to fascinate people and institutions all around the world. Presidential campaigns are often heated, nasty, expensive and exhaustive, but the spirit of nationalism always prevails on election night. The result, except in the cases of John Quincy Adams and George W. Bush which took some time to resolve, unites and rallies the people around America's national interest and security.

In this book, I have attempted to present the presidents in a historical, social and political context. It is a context in which the personal history of each President reveals the diversity of the nation and its maturation process. Presidents are people with strengths and weaknesses, but they are often deified as superhumans by the public. The starting point of a meaningful presidency is for us to see our presidents as human beings with strengths and weaknesses.

John Adams once noted that his children gave him more pain than all of his enemies. If we develop this mindset, the service and commitment of our presidents will be both practical and meaningful to us.

It is my ardent hope that the insights provided in this book, *The American Presidents: George Washington to Abraham Lincoln*, will enhance our understanding and appreciation of our American heritage.

George Washington

George Washington was the first President of the United States. He was tempted to become a military dictator and a powerful king, but he refused. Washington chose the good of his country and the interest of his people above personal power and selfish advancement. The statement, "First in war, first in peace and first in the hearts of his countrymen," gives a vivid description of the immense influence of Mr. Washington on the lives of the American nation and people. General Henry Lee made the above statement as a tribute to Washington when he spoke to Congress after Washington's death.

Washington had no ambition for the presidency; what he really wanted was to live and die an honest man on his own farm. However, the good of his country and the influence of his supporters led him to run for the office of president. He successfully and easily won the election. He received all the electoral votes allotted for a presidential candidate, and they were sixty-nine. John Adams received thirty-four electoral votes and became Vice President.

American political journeys regarding elections of leaders for the country are different. The elected government officials, at different levels of the nation, are elected by the people of their designated political district or state. The President and Vice President of the United States of America are elected by a select group of citizens known as members of the Electoral College. Each member of the Electoral College is pledged to vote for one of the presidential candidates. In this light, when a citizen casts a vote for a presidential candidate, he or she is actually voting for an "elector." The presidential election is never concluded until the electors meet and vote for the candidates they are pledged to. After this exercise, the President and Vice President are declared as duly elected to serve the nation in their respective capacities. During this period, New York City was the capital of the United States, but after serving from New York for a year, Washington and his wife moved to Philadelphia, the new U.S. capital.

The District of Columbia was established by an act of the United States Congress in 1791 as the new capital. As a sign of respect and tribute to George Washington for his tireless services to the nation and its people, the new capital was named in his honor. This is why we call the capital city Washington D.C. In 1793, Washington himself laid the cornerstone for the U.S. capital building. This action by Washington is still a very significant milestone in American democracy.

That Washington was the hero of the Revolution shows his commitment to the well-being of his country. He became a very popular man after the Revolution. His noted popularity and devotion became an open invitation that could have easily made him a powerful and popular dictator. The people gave him vast presidential power, but he chose the path of promoting a strong legislative branch of government. He saw a weak presidency with a national focus as good system of government for the people, by the people and of the people.

There was concern by some of the people in the early days of the country that history might repeat itself if the government was too powerful. They were afraid that the new government would become too strong and too powerful at the expense of individual rights and freedoms. Washington saw the Chief Executive as one who seeks the greater good and best interest of the entire nation and citizenry.

Will Cleveland and Mark Alvarez, in their book, *Yo, Millard Fillmore!*, wrote that Washington was so popular after the Revolution he could have assumed the powers of a dictator. But this was far from Washington's beliefs and values. It is widely believed that, although he could easily have been elected to a third term as president, he declined to run. He felt the new country's success and greatness depended on its ideals, its laws and its representative form of government. American democracy is noble and cherished because Washington demonstrated that his personal leadership, or that of others, did not matter.

Washington established a peaceful transfer of power from one President to the next. His example presented the nation the opportunity to treat government in the context of the people's interests. He certainly was a man of great honor, dignity, courage and principle. His devotion to the future and freedom of his country provided him an historical spotlight that honors him as the greatest of all American heroes.

Washington endured the rough times of life. He had disastrous experiences during his very first military command. The site he chose to build a fortification known as Fort Necessary, near what we know as Pittsburgh, PA, was considered by many accounts the worst possible of all sites during the French and Indian War. He was left with no choice but to surrender the site to the French. This, with other experiences of the Revolution, might have made Washington very discouraged, but he never gave up on his goal for a great and unified America.

Washington was a public man of decisive action. As a young legislator in the Virginia House of Burgesses, he manifested visible stage fright in making speeches, but he was resolute in reaching decisions. He was initially a mere spectator who watched the mounting tension that took place between America and Great Britain as he managed his Virginia plantation. His later decision to become a part of the resistance led to him being elected a member of the Continental Congress.

What we know as the Eastern United States was, in the 1770s, a colony of England. The people in this area were under the rule of England, and they paid taxes to the British government. Their ruler was not a president but King George III. This made some of the people very mad, but others who were happy to be part of England. Those who were mad started talking about breaking away from England and organizing a separate government. These people mounted a vigorous protest known as the Revolutionary War, and they took George Washington as their military leader.

Washington was made commander of the American forces at Cambridge, and he was fully in charge of the military operations of the Revolution. As Commander in Chief, he was responsible to put together an army and train soldiers and to ask the new government for food, guns, clothing and other logistics for his men. Operating an army with poor shelter, very little food and cold weather made the battle extremely difficult for Washington and his men.

The troops became re-energized to fight when the new government finally responded to Washington's plea by providing more food and supplies. Prior to this, the army stayed in Valley Forge, Pennsylvania. In Valley Forge, the soldiers seriously suffered because of the cold. Another factor in their suffering was that they did not have enough food.

Washington might not have been the greatest military planner, but he had common sense and determination. He had the will to win, and he inspired his men to do the same. He was made Commander of the colonial army in Virginia and fought in fierce battles against the French and the Indians. This was remarkable for a young man, and it provided experiences useful for the greater battle against Great Britain.

It is recorded that for seven years, Washington was in the field of New England that gave him victory at Boston. He was, however, defeated on Long Island, harried down through New Jersey, imprisoned by winter at Valley Forge and driven by unfailing will through to the end at Yorktown. He was on a mission to claim America for Americans and to create a nation of freedom for all people.

Washington steadfastly refused, at any time, to risk all on a single throw of the dice. He was criticized by some of the people for his inaction. There were others who accused him for his timidity. Washington managed to hold the revolutionary army together and inspire confidence in the civilians until the struggle was brought to a triumphant finish. When the war was over, the victorious General surrendered his authority to the Congress and retired to his home at Mount Vernon.

For example, the Revolutionary War was fought in many areas of the eastern United States. For example, they were fought in Massachusetts, New York, New Jersey and Pennsylvania. The British forces finally surrendered to Washington and his troops at Yorktown, Pennsylvania after six years of intense battle. The significance of this victory by the continental army under the able command of Superior General George Washington is the independence it won for the United States.

In 1789, George Washington was sworn in as the first President of the newly formed United States of America. The American colonies had finally won their independence from Great Britain in the Revolutionary War. Washington was not only a hero of the War that liberated his beloved nation, he was a symbol of freedom and democracy for the new republic. Washington therefore became everyone's first choice as president, and he governed well.

Washington was a wise, good and great man who spent time personally helping to resolve differences between high ranking members of his administration. For example, when tension between his Secretary of State, Thomas Jefferson, and his Secretary of the Treasury, Alexander Hamilton, got very high, Washington mediated between both men. Washington displayed wisdom and moderation in launching the new United States' government which had much to accomplish before it could win the respect of nations such as Great Britain, France and Spain. Americans had chosen their ideal leader. Washington's example defined the presidency for all time.

Washington always felt that he was an ordinary citizen serving his country in whatever role he was assigned or elected to. He saw his life in politics as similar to his life in the military. Washington was on the front line of defense for the heart and soul of America. He never wanted to desert his country in its greatest time of need. In their book, *The American President*, Philip B. Kunhardt Jr., Philip B. Kunhardt III and Peter W. Kunhardt described Washington as a person who fought for the freedom of his country.

Washington made his farewell address in 1796 and announced his intention to retire at the end of his second term as president. He underscored the importance of national unity as the "main pillar" of the nation's independence, peace and prosperity. He was critical of partisan political squabbling and taught the people to be natural and open to foreign nations and foreign affairs.

John Adams

 John Adams had more formal education than George Washington, but he had far less status as a leader. He was an honest man and a strong supporter of the values dear to Washington's heart and soul, but he was cranky, vain, condescending, self-righteous and short-tempered throughout his life. He made no secret of these characteristics when he called himself "puffy, vain, conceited." He gloried in vanity as a noble part of his life, and he succeeded in getting his peers to agree with him.

He was a unassuming politician who made people with whom he joined forces unsure of what side he was on. Nevertheless, they were delighted to have such incorruptible, extraordinarily intelligent and courageous personality on their side. He loved books and gathered enough to make a lasting impact. His large collection of books was left to the Boston Public Library after his death. He was deeply in love with his books, his family and his fireside, but he had some reluctance about politics.

Adams was committed to the independence of his country. To a great extent, he was also committed to the religious, social and political rights of others. He came from a Puritan religious background and skillfully reconstructed this past into a republican beginning. Explaining his revolutionary approach, he once noted that it was a love for universal liberty that actually projected, conducted and accomplished the settlement of America.

The Puritan ideal of moving to Massachusetts Bay was not for religious and political freedom but simply to worship the way they pleased. The Puritan presence in Massachusetts Bay was responsible for congregations, schools, militia and town meetings. This presence engulfed their community in a unique way and left an imprint on the lives of the people. John Adams was no exception.

Adams came from a background in which he regarded God as the central point of life. He used his Calvinistic doctrine of human nature to inspire a republican vision. Adams saw worship as the central purpose of the Puritan movement, but he also saw religious and political freedom as elements that were immensely important to America.

Adams taught that the American Revolution was actually a continuation under new auspices of an old quest for a pure and righteous commonwealth. He believed that the period of the Enlightenment missed its mark by seeking to replace the central role of God in human affairs with man and nature. Religion was a foundation for a country to be built on, and its role should be enhanced with the growth of the nation, not eliminated.

John Adams was born on a small farm near what is now Quincy, Massachusetts. It is believed that his parents were not well educated, but they sent him to Harvard University.

Adams taught school briefly, then studied law. It is also believed that, when he heard a speech in 1761 by James Otis, it made an imprint on his life. Otis was speaking against a law passed by the British parliament and said the law was unfair because the colonies had no one in parliament to speak against it. Mr. Otis argued that if a law was unfair and unjust, the people had a right to oppose it. He taught that the people had the right to make their own laws.

As a young man, Adams was deeply moved by the practical speech of Mr. Otis. He identified this as a primary reason his parents moved to America. They were in favor of the freedom for individuals to make their own laws. Adams believed in liberty with his whole heart.

Adams was a student of law, philosophy, history and literature. He wanted to build an opportunity for the freedom of people. A commitment to freedom, liberty, justice and fair play were cherished elements in Adams' life. He had first-hand information about the people's desire for freedom from Great Britain and personal experience as an active partner in the liberation movement. He was a true freedom fighter whose brave, stubborn and honest characteristics secured him a unique place in American and world history.

Adams was in the first group of people to support the idea of American independence. He admired Washington and supported him as a military and political leader. John Adams might have been smarter than Washington, and just as honest, but he was also cranky, vain and no great a leader of people. He is credited as one of the earliest persons to come out in favor of American independence.

It was Adams who nominated Washington to command American forces in the Revolution. He helped to negotiate the peace treaty that made the United States a sovereign nation. He earnestly served as Washington's Vice President for eight years. Adams had great integrity, but he didn't have the ability to make people like him, and this manifested itself in the fact that he was never a popular President in his own right.

Cleveland and Alvarez write that Adams was from Massachusetts—the only non-Virginian among our first five presidents—and that he was the first to live in the White House. They also record that the building wasn't finished when he and his wife, Abigail, moved in. Abigail, they note, could find nowhere suitable to dry their laundry, so she hung it up in the East Room which is now the site of state dinners and receptions. Adam died at ninety, the longest living of all our presidents.

Adams, as earlier stated, came from a Puritan background. He had exposure to local political activism and was a product of colonial farmers. His political journey started when he committed himself to the cause of American independence. He was the kind of law maker whose legislative posture transcended the issues that emotionally involved his fellow patriots.

Adams once noted that, "It was not religion alone as is commonly supposed but it was the love of universal liberty that projected, conducted and accomplished the Settlement of America." He also noted, during his second night in the White House, "I pray Heaven to bestow the best Blessings on this House and all that shall hereafter inhabit it. May None but honest and wise men ever rule beneath this roof."

During the time when Adams became president, Great Britain and France were at war. Despite the neutrality of the United States, the French attacked U.S. ships to prevent them from trading with Great Britain. Adams ordered the building of warships as a preparatory and preventive strategy against a possible war with the French. In a proactive move, he established a naval department and ordered war ships to be built.

The battle at sea went on between the French and United States frigates for some two years without a formal declaration of war between the two countries. Adams was truly the father of the United States Navy. This was truly an historic and outstanding accomplishment for the Adams administration.

Michael Beschloss, in the book, *The American Heritage*, writes that John Adams was not born into the first family of the United States; he founded it. I believe the point being made is that his Puritan ancestors were active in local affairs. The record of the Adamses of Massachusetts remained typical colonial farmers until John and Susanna Boylston Adams of Braintree parish had their first son. Young Adams was born on October 30, 1735. In his early years, Adams developed a brilliance of intellect and a uniqueness of character that he passed to his children and succeeding generations. John Adams' character separated him from his forefathers and distinguished him from his descendants. The Adamses undoubtedly became a part of the heart and soul of American.

Adams was a man very dedicated to the cause of freedom and those religious contributions responsible for the republic's freedom. He was also a very open-minded man who was a member of the group that wrote the Declaration of Independence. In this document, it is stated that all men are born equal and free. It states that people have the right to revolt against those who will not give them freedom.

Some people dismissed any dialogue about the institutional injustice of slavery. They make the historic claim that the time and condition merited the practices of slavery and unfair treatment of Blacks and Indians. The least and last of society are the forgotten people whose concerns are often overlooked.

Institutionalized slavery, colonialism and apartheid are the modern kinship of state-sponsored terrorism because they dehumanize, kill, destroy and victimize the innocent. They divide people and indiscriminately subject people of all ages to present and lasting pain and damage. Another set of factors to take into consideration is individual hated and oppression. Too often, these factors transcend racial, ethnic, social and religious lines. We are all guilty, at one point or another, of prejudice and shortsightedness, but we can all make a difference.

Injustice and slavery are wrong, but we must live in the reality that history does not change because of our disagreement with it. We have to transcend the ugly past, heal our wounds and unite our efforts to make the Declaration of Independence applicable to all people regardless of race, creed, gender or nationality. There is nothing wrong with the Declaration of Independence; the problem is the failure to apply it to all people.

John Adams actually developed interest in politics when he started to work as a lawyer. The Stamp Act actually angered him. This was a British tax system that forced the colonists to pay extra tax on things like newspapers, legal papers, and, in some cases, taxes were imposed on playing cards. Adams responded by writing articles in newspapers against the Stamp Acts. His publications elevated him in the minds of many as an important thinker and writer in the cause of freedom.

He was committed to scholarship, and this was seen throughout his career, especially in his "Boston Instructions." The farmer's letters won a deep place in John's heart, and he spent a great amount of time reading them aloud to his wife, Abigail. The letters were warm and reasonable. They were written by John Dickinson of Pennsylvania and had attracted such great attention that they were being widely printed. Dickinson was more a scholar and a gentleman with a London education and a handsome fortune than a farmer. He took the time to write in an idiom, plain and beautiful, that the country could understand. He wrote that a perpetual jealousy respecting liberty is absolutely prerequisite in all free states, adding that liberty is never exposed to so much danger as when the people believe there is the least.

There was a series of debates about party politics during his administration. People in his administration were concerned about what the role of government should be. This led to the formation of two political parties. The Federalists, under the leadership of Alexander Hamilton, held the view that there should be a strong central government that protected the interests of landowners and industrialists. The Democratic-Republicans, under the leadership of Thomas Jefferson, held the view that states should be given the rights to decide on matters relating to their own local needs. In spite of his election as a Federalist, Adams was the truest example of a centralist president.

As his health began to decline, he decided, with the help of his wife, to leave public life. He had shared with his wife that his health was failing, and felt he was going into decline. He told her how difficult it was for him to make a speech in court because his chest hurt and his throat would tighten as if someone closed a hand around it. John told his wife that his flesh was failing so rapidly, he had scarce strength enough to mount a horse. He felt the need to put things in order because he was about to leave the world.

Abigail assured him he was not dying and suggested he needed some rest. To drive her point home, she told him that his legs were looking very well and shared how she had always admired his legs. As a farsighted wife, Abigail advised her husband to travel away from city life and return home to Braintree. She felt the source of his problem was his many friends who were misleading him. They had been tearing at him like wolves. Therefore, Abigail advised that if they left town and town politics, he would be able to breathe freely and benefit greatly from the atmosphere of country life.

John Adams spent his days in retirement reading and writing. He admired and read the writings of Sam Adams who, five weeks after the massacre trials in Boston, had launched a series of articles in the Gazette signed "Vindex." In these carefully, suavely and venomous articles, Sam Adams presented what he considered proof that the soldier should have been hanged. The result of his articles was that a new trial was ordered and, to a great extent, Sam Adams became judge, jury and council for the persecution.

John Adams was fascinated by these articles and spent much time reading them. He was moved by how Vindex recalled that, as the trials opened, defense counsel took the pains to quote from the English law a phrase directed at the prisoners: "May God send you a good deliverance...." It was same prayer Vindex now made for the three juries: "On their own day of trial before the Eternal Judge, may God send them good deliverance." John Adams loved these words. He quoted them and was willing to risk his life for them, but when a delegation headed by Sam

Adams asked him to serve as orator at the anniversary of the Boston Massacre, John Adams declined the invitation on grounds that he was out of politics for good.

The welcoming hands of death visited both Adams and Jefferson on July 4, 1826 when America was celebrating its jubilee—the fiftieth anniversary of independence. John Adams died that day at age ninety and, on the same day before sunset in Virginia, Thomas Jefferson died. The second and third presidents died at a time of celebration for the freedom and stability that characterized America. They both had fought hard to ensure America became the greatest nation on earth. They lived to see it happen, and they died when the nation was celebrating their investment and the efforts of all Americans who sacrificed time, effort and their lives for the greater good of their country.

Thomas Jefferson

 Thomas Jefferson is noted for being one of the authors of the Declaration of Independence and the founder of the University of Virginia. As president, his administration added the Louisiana territory to the United States. The United States bought the territory and doubled the size of the nation. Jefferson succeeded in purchasing lands that doubled the size of the United States. This deal is known as the Louisiana Purchase. The United States paid fifteen million dollars to France. It actually averaged around three cents an acre. The lands that were purchased ranged from the Mississippi River to the Rocky Mountains and from the Canadian border to Texas.

Jefferson was an educator whose interest in brilliant minds and talented people is almost unmatched by that of any other U.S. president. He explored the theory and practice of agriculture, architecture and zoology. He also developed the concept of micro-economics. When he came to the Revolution, Jefferson, as a Virginian, was alienated from the traditional religious culture of his own community.

Jefferson was on the committee that formulated the Declaration of Independence. He and John Adams, with probably some others, were assigned to write a draft of the document. It is believed that Jefferson had praised and hailed the knowledge of his friend John Adams. He wrote the final document and credited himself for some of John Adams' knowledge and contributions. This was very disappointing to Adams, and it almost cost them their friendship. For a long time, these two men exchanged some harsh criticisms of each other, but in their later years, they regained their friendship and respect for each other. The letters and praise they exchanged are some of the best testimonies of great American minds.

The need for religion to occupy a central place in human affairs was not given any consideration, and he articulated that human destiny was controlled by nature and not providence. This, for Jefferson, proved that man was inherently good, seeking his own happiness through the happiness of others. He believed that nature, through the progress of knowledge, would answer all of its questions.

The idea of separation of church and state came from Jefferson. He did not feel that church discipline and teaching should be a requirement because civil education was the sole requirement. The hope of heaven and the fear of hell were unnecessary religious restraints, and it would be unjust for them to be supported by civil government.

Thomas Jefferson wrote, "...that truth advances and error recedes step by step only, and to do our fellow men the most good in our power, we must lead where we can, follow where we cannot, and still go with them, watching always the favorable moment for helping them to another great step." After reviewing the synopsis, he once confided in Charles Thomson, the great evangelist and author, that he too had made a "wee little book" from the same materials which he called, "The Philosophy of Jesus." Jefferson was religious but he taught that the line of operation between religion and the state should be separate and distinct.

Thomas Jefferson was a student of law, history, philosophy and literature who wanted to build a personal library. In the end, his personal library, which numbered over six thousand volumes, was sold to Congress in 1815. This library became the nucleus of the Library of Congress. He was reluctant to become a politician, but, in his fight for what he wanted America to be like, he accepted the challenge to enter politics.

Jefferson was academically powerful. He was a man with both brain and power. His interest in knowledge went with him to the White House. He was a disloyal Vice President to John Adams because he felt himself more educated than Adams. Jefferson could not take directives from Adams because he felt it undermined his cherished academic advantage over Adams. Adams' response was to always complain about the self- seeking attitude of Jefferson. It was clear to Adams that Jefferson had a different goal—the office of president. The system for electing a Vice President during this period of American history was different from what we have today. In Jefferson's day, the person with the next highest vote was selected Vice President. He had no party ties and did not necessarily support the vision and policies of the president.

In his inaugural address of 1801, Jefferson made his famous reference to the United States as "the world's best hope" and his praise of "wise and frugal government, which shall retain men from injuring one another, (and) shall leave them otherwise free to regulate their own pursuits." His electoral victory over John Adams marked the first real change of party control and made his promise to respect the rights of the federalist minority seen the most important point in his address.

Jefferson helped develop the monetary system used in the United States and the system by which territories became states in the new republic. He was the champion of many outstanding causes that continued to develop the nation.

Jefferson's career was a success of triumphs, and he carved a niche in history by moving from one success story to another. He began in 1774 as a gifted local politician who went on to serve in the Continental Congress at the urging of his friends. After completing his law studies in 1767, Jefferson began to practice law in Williamsburg, the capital city of Virginia at the time. His interest led him to visit the Virginia House of Burgesses to hear debates, and in 1769 he was elected to the Virginia House of Burgesses.

Later in his career, Jefferson became the Minister to France. This was a crucial point in American life, especially as a new republic. Jefferson was the point man for United States trade ties with the countries of Europe. He successfully masterminded many trade agreements between the United States and other European nations. During the five years he spent in France, Jefferson benefited from the arts, music, agriculture and architecture. He was the Governor of Virginia during the Revolutionary War and the first Secretary of State. He had a growing passion for politics, but even the position of Vice

President did not stop his passion. He accomplished his vision, becoming a two-term President and the historic third President of the United States.

In a heated election battle with President John Adams, Jefferson failed to win the popular vote and in 1801, for the first time, the Electoral College decided the outcome of the presidential election. The second time this happened was in 1825 for John Quincy Adams, and George W. Bush was the third person to have benefited from this exercise. In the case of George W. Bush, the heavy involvement of the United States Supreme Court left the impression on some voters that it was the court that actually determined the outcome of the election.

George Bush's democratic opponent, Albert Gore, who was also Vice President to Bill Clinton, put the matter to rest when he announced the outcome of the Electoral College and told the entire nation that George W. Bush was the President the people had elected to serve the country. I was so elated with the spirit of nationalism, I shared with Tim Mabbitt, Pastor of First Christian Church, my impression and admiration of American democracy. In many parts of the world, immediate or civil war would have overtaken nationalism. Such shortsightedness often destroys the nation and the future of its people. This is an American tradition that many nations of the world must adapt and practice. George W. Bush was the third person in U.S. history to have benefited from this process, and he is the President of the United States.

Thomas Jefferson made history by being the author of the Declaration of Independence and serving as the cofounder of the Democratic Party. In 1854, the Republican Party chose their name to honor his commitment to the proposition "that all men are created equal." He was a very popular president during his two terms because he cut taxes and government spending.

James Madison

The son of a planter and a homemaker, James Madison was born in the home of his maternal grandmother at Port Conway, Virginia, on March 16, 1751. Like George Washington and Thomas Jefferson, Madison was a true product of a powerful planter aristocracy. Madison transcended the stereotype of what a large family can do or cannot do. He grew up on Montpelier, a place built by his father, James Madison Sr., and named his family seat. On this farm was a two-story frame house where he grew up—the firstborn of his family. When one reads about Madison, there is a deep-rooted history in professional areas like carpentry, tobacco farming, general farming and homemaking.

At age eighteen, he enrolled at Princeton University, then known as the College of New Jersey. His commitment to studies led him to complete the four-year academic requirements in two years. There were times he had only five hours of sleep at night because he had combined his junior and senior years. He passed his final exams in 1771 but was too sick to attend his own graduation.

The influence of his mother and grandmother on his academic journey is vital for today's parents with similar challenges. Madison's life experience with his mother and grandmother reveal the vital role of women in nation building. They taught him how to read and write. They produced a president who was widely respected as the nation builder.

Madison had the odds against him, but he also had the will to succeed. He was five feet, four inches tall, prematurely bald and had a squeaky voice. These physical challenges might have contributed to what President John F. Kennedy referred to when he remarked, "James Madison is our most underrated president." But Madison, during all of his public life, was able to win the respect of his peers, especially when he rose to speak.

As a student of arts and government, Madison served in council chamber, in the Virginia legislature and the Continental Congress. He was an informed mind who pushed for a stronger union. Unlike Washington and Hamilton who faced steel on the battlefield, Madison had served in politics. His early participation in the movement for a stronger Union culminated in a constitutional convention. He helped draw up a new plan of government and toiled assiduously as a delegate at the convention. He also helped to stamp needed political philosophy upon its thought and made careful notes of the proceedings. As a member of the first Congress, he aided in putting the federal government to work.

Madison was both a bookish man and a conversationalist of great knowledge and wit. He was also a very practical and satirical man. As a scholar, he would have preferred good discussions with his friend Thomas Jefferson on

Greek philosophy and its applicability to American politics. But he also felt the need to engage his wife's guests in small talk, charming them with his ingratiating smile and wry jests. He had an open personality that related to people of all social and political settings.

Madison served Thomas Jefferson for eight years as Secretary of State. Strictly speaking, Madison was both a politician and a social philosopher. He was deeply into the motives of mankind, especially economic motives. Exploring the past, he developed class conflict. He was busy everywhere. He looked forward into the future.

Madison was small in stature, mild in manner, diffident and introspective. He was poorly equipped for the rough and tumble of politics but still rolled on to success. He brought alive the concept that all Americans are equal. Madison actually gave the nation the opportunity to reflect on the hidden values of equal opportunity. America is still growing into this ideal, but it is recognizing the rights of all people in ways never heard of in its historical journey.

Madison was a key player in the drafting, negotiating and defending of the American constitution. It took an outsider with little reputation in statute like Madison to make a difference in American democracy. Madison created a skillful revolution that advanced the American nation. He was given the nickname, "the Father of the Constitution." Madison believed in the greatness of his country, and he celebrated it beyond expectation. For example, when the British captured Washington and burned the White House in 1812 during his presidency, his many opponents called the war, "Mr. Madison's War."

As the shortest and smallest President (he weighed about 100 pounds), Madison demonstrated to the nation that the White House is truly the People's House and is therefore no respecter of stature. He transformed the American presidential political landscape because he had a mind and will that transcended his appearance.

His wife, Dolley Madison, stood by her man in all senses of commitment and became a national hero. Mrs. Madison is known as the first person to serve ice cream at the White House. She was a popular figure in Washington who received votes on the floor of the House of Representatives after the death of her husband. She also defended freedom by risking her life in the interest of American freedom. In her capacity as the First Lady, she escaped just before the British arrived. Mrs. Madison was able to take with her the famous Stuart portrait of George Washington. Without her heroic action, this historic investment would have been totally destroyed.

James Madison held a more elevated view toward the office of Vice President than most people. Unlike the office of the President, in which the constitution made provision for the President to receive compensation for his services, there was no similar position for the Vice President.

During the first Congress, the issue of whether the Vice President should get a salary did come to the floor. The views were both diverse and complex. Some members of the House of Representatives held the view that the Vice President should be paid on a daily basis because he would have so little to do. Madison viewed this as an offense to the dignity of the second office of the government. He pushed for the Vice President to be given an annual salary which was accepted, and an annual salary of 5,000 dollars was finally agreed upon. Madison had seen the disadvantages of the office occupied by Vice President, and he wanted to do something about honoring it. The distinction was seen from the start. For example, the Presidential Oath was historically administered by the Chief Justices, but the Oath of the Vice President had been administered by various officials of government. Prior to 1860, the Oath for Vice President was administered by the temporary President.

After 1860, the Vice Presidential Oath was administered by either the outgoing Vice President, Senate Party Leader, a Supreme Court Justice or the Speaker of the House Representatives.

Madison's emphasis on the dignity of the second office opened the debate that helped people viewed the Vice President as a partner to the President. Since 1837, when the changes to the Twelfth Amendment were followed for the first time, the President will take his oath first and then the Vice President. Both men are sworn in in the portico of the Capitol. Prior to this, the President usually took his oath in the senate chamber. After this ceremony, the newly elected Vice President would be sworn in on the portico, the balcony in the front of the Capitol.

Madison's dream for a dignified second office has truly come alive in the last thirty plus years. The Vice President now has an executive on the grounds of the Naval Observatory in Washington, D.C. He has become an active player in the administration's affairs, given a large staff, gets protection from Secret Service agents, has his own seal and flag and offices in the Capitol, the Senate office building and the executive office building.

James Madison was pleased about the revolutionary changes that continued to elevate and dignify the second office.

James Monroe

 James Monroe was born in Westmoreland County, Virginia on April 28, 1758. He was the oldest of five children and was brought up in a highly charged political household. His father, Spence Monroe, was a hard-working farmer, and his mother, Elizabeth Jones Monroe, was a homemaker, but politics was a major topic of conversation in their household.

Young Monroe served his country as a soldier in the War of Independence. By the time he was ready for college life, talk of independence for the United States was rapidly spreading across America. In 1774 when he entered college, the first Continental Congress was starting its historic meeting in Philadelphia. He was only eighteen when he left college and joined the army. He was committed to fighting for the independence of his beloved country and fought in several of the major battles.

At twenty years of age, he was given a group of soldiers to command and proved himself a brave and effective soldier. The new Lieutenant marched north with the Third Virginia

Regiment to join General George Washington's army in New York. Monroe was wounded in the Battle of Harlem Heights in 1776 after Washington retreated from New York City, but he was able to barely escape the enemies' fire.

When the American troops crossed the ice-filled Delaware River on Christmas Eve, it was Monroe who led an advance team into the enemy camp. This caught the Hessian troops, hired by the British to fight for them, by great surprise. Commander Monroe was wounded in the shoulder, but he still kept command of his team until the enemy finally surrendered.

James Monroe was the last patriot of the revolutionary era to become President. He became President during one of the most fortunate periods in American history. This period is significant because it was after the early settlement of the disputes of the United States and before the serious disputes between the North and the South. In the language of today, Monroe would have been regarded "a lucky guy." His administration declared it would not allow any European countries to further colonize North and South America. This policy is known as the "Monroe Doctrine."

In December 1823, Monroe took a bold step by announcing his foreign policy to the world. He made it clear that the United States would no longer look kindly on European nations that tried to interfere in North and South American affairs. He also warned against any new attempts to establish colonies in the Americas by European powers.

Monroe was a close associate of Thomas Jefferson. He was a law student of Jefferson who inspired him to get involve in politics. Jefferson's impression of Monroe as a very bright and able student opened many doors of opportunity for the young man. He was educated at William and

Mary but his political philosophy conveys more of George Washington than Thomas Jefferson or James Madison.

Monroe chose the path of active political life and government service over that of practicing country lawyer. He was elected to Congress along with Thomas Jefferson and James Madison. These three Virginians remained close friends and allies throughout the genesis stages of the new nation. Towards the end of his term in Congress, Monroe met and married Elizabeth Kortwright, daughter of a New York merchant. He returned to Virginia with his wife and opened a law office in Fredericksburg. Monroe did not find life very appealing in that part of the country.

Monroe was an active player in the negotiation of the Louisiana territory purchased from France that doubled the size of the United States. He was a career diplomat and skillful politician. These qualities and his friendship with James Madison led to him being named to two positions, Secretary of State and Secretary of War during the Madison administration. Madison needed his experience in local, national and international politics at a time when the nation was faced with great challenges. President Madison needed a loyal and capable ally like Monroe to move his agenda in a more positive direction. Monroe was a political ally whose view and integrity Madison highly respected.

When Monroe was elected a delegate in 1788 to a Virginia convention called to ratify the new Constitution of the United States, he took an opposing position to his friend Madison, known as the father of the Constitution. Monroe's opposition was predicated on the grounds that the new Constitution did not contain a Bill of Rights for the protection of private citizens. After the Virginia convention narrowly approved the new Constitution, he accepted the result and began working towards the formation of a new government. He lost to Madison the election to the New House of Representatives, but both men developed a great sense of respect for each other and an outstanding loyalty to the freedom of their country.

Monroe had vast experience in politics and government. He was one of the principle actors in President James Madison's administration. He provided helpful advice to Madison on how to handle problems with other nations. In 1812, when the United States went to war against England, the international experience of Secretary of State Monroe became crucial to Madison.

Monroe was Secretary of State and a civilian when the demoralized American troops fled from the British force that landed in Chesapeake Bay and started to march on Washington in 1814. He immediately stepped in and organized a defense for the capital. His efforts failed, and the British captured Washington, burning both the Capitol building and the White House. To deal with England's superior naval power and to allow America the freedom of movement on the sea, Madison also made Monroe Secretary of War. He was named Secretary while serving as the Secretary of State. This historic nontraditional move by President Madison made Monroe the first man in American history to have served in two Cabinet positions at the same time.

When Monroe became Secretary of War, he confronted a threat by the British in New Orleans by sending General Andrew Jackson to command the American troops in that area. He also sent a message to the governors of the western states to hasten their militia to New Orleans, adding that every man should bring his own rifle. His plan worked, and General Jackson succeeded in commanding a force of American sharpshooters who mowed down the British redcoats as they advanced towards New Orleans. It was a great American victory that made Jackson and Monroe national heroes.

Monroe had a burden to unify the country, and he invested time and resources in getting the job done. As presidential candidate of the Democratic-Republican Party for the election of 1816, the nation turned to him for national leadership, and he won with an overwhelming victory. He was inaugurated as the fifth President of the United States on March 4, 1817, shortly before his fifty-ninth birthday. Realizing that the nation was at peace both at home and abroad, he said at his inauguration, "Never did a government commence under auspices so favorable."

Within the first three months of his presidency, he left Washington D.C. for a tour of the middle and northern United States. He told the nation that he wanted to inspect the federal shipyards, the ports and frontier outposts. But he also wanted to use his appearance as a means of restoring national unity damaged by the recent war. He also took into account the characterization of his political opponent, Rufus King of New York, who said Monroe "had the zealous support of nobody, and he was exempt from the hostility of everybody." Monroe's strategy was to show that the American people uncompromisingly supported his style of leadership and policies.

The trip succeeded beyond the widest imagination of Monroe himself. The roadsides and riverbanks were filled with people anxious to have a glimpse of him, and cheering crowds greeted his arrival at state capitals. He recounted his experience in a letter to Thomas Jefferson: "In principal towns the whole population has been in motion, and in a manner to produce the greatest of excitement possible."

Monroe's presidency was recorded as the "Era of Good Feelings." The country was enjoying political and domestic tranquility. It was a time of peace with favorable global conditions. There was a depression in 1819, and the next year the Missouri Compromise ignited angry debates about the extension of slavery in the new states and territories. These created some rough paths for the Monroe administration, but they did not undermine the good feelings prevailing in the country during the Monroe era.

James Monroe is best remembered for his famous foreign policy doctrine known as the "Monroe Doctrine." The eight years Monroe served as President, he had some memorable experiences such as the great business panic that broke in 1819. This event shook the economic structure of western civilization by foreshadowing similar disturbances in the capitalist system. The following year (1820-21), with Monroe's approval, Congress affected the famous Missouri Compromise between slavery and freedom that was viewed as a win-win situation for each side. Missouri was admitted to the Union as a slave state and Maine as a free state. The remaining Louisiana territory was divided into free and slave regions by the parallel of thirty-six degrees and thirty inches. Monroe concluded the negotiations with Spain in 1821 for Florida and made it a part of the territorial heritage of the American Republic.

John Quincy Adams

John Quincy Adams was a servant of his people and country. At the age of fourteen he went to Russia as Secretary to the United States Minister. His early exposure to politics and government provided him the opportunity to develop a career of service that was characterized by selflessness and intelligent devotion.

Until the election of George W. Bush, Adams held the distinguished role of being the only President who was the son of a president. His style of governance and his personality were greatly influenced by his father, John Adams. Frank Freidel, in his book, *Our Country's Presidents*, writes, "Adams was the only president who was the son of a president, and in many respects his career as well as his temperament and viewpoints paralleled those of his famous father."

America for the first time witnessed a very strange turn of history in which the son of a president became President of the nation. John Adams was actually humiliated and driven from power by the Republicans, but his son John

Quincy, in the midst of it, left his father's party and joined the Jeffersonians. This change of strategy energized John Quincy's desire for the higher office of the land. It is unclear if his desire for the presidency was to redeem his father's reputation by those who had humiliated him or to simply prove a point that the Adams were good for America. He did not win the popular ballots or the electoral votes against Andrew Jackson but by calculative and manipulative means: the House of Representatives, responsible for the outcome of the elections, named John Quincy President.

John Quincy was not as popular a leader as Andrew Jackson, but he had name recognition. His noble accomplishments and achievements could not connect with the voters in an age when frontier democracy was flooding into Washington, a thirst for power and office. The outcome of the elections by the House of Representatives hunted John Quincy and probably undermined the integrity of presidency during his administration.

The election itself was honest. It involved four important candidates in the Electoral College, and Andrew Jackson got most of the votes but not enough to win him the presidency. The result of the election was placed in the hands of the House of Representatives. John Quincy became President. Jackson and his supporters felt that crooked deals by John Quincy had deprived them of the opportunity to win the presidency.

Adams was born in Braintree, Massachusetts on July 11, 1767. His mother, Abigail, witnessed with him the historic Battle of Bunker Hill from the top of Penn's Hill above the family farm. He grew up during the Revolutionary War, and he was only seven years old when the Declaration of Independence was signed. At the age of ten, John Quincy went to France with his father, John Adams, who was sent to France to win their support for the Revolutionary War.

John Quincy used the advantage of his presence in Europe to become an accomplished linguist. He learned and became versed in French, Greek, Latin and Dutch. His knowledge and ability led President George Washington to appoint him as United States Ambassador to the Netherlands. It was a great honor for him to have been appointed the chief spokesman for his government at the age of twenty-eight.

John Quincy was also appointed by his father as ambassador to Prussia and was named the first American Ambassador to Russia by James Madison. During his service in Russia, the war between England and America started in 1812. He worked on the Treaty of Ghent, the peace treaty that ended the war in 1814. In 1814, he was appointed Ambassador to Great Britain.

John Quincy became James Monroe's chief foreign advisor and diplomat. As Secretary of State, he became the champion of problem solving between America and the rest of the world. He articulated the foreign policy of his country in such a way that he is remembered as one of the most important Secretaries of State in American history. When Florida and most of western America belonged to Spain, he convinced Spain to turn over Florida and most of northwestern America to the United States. His successful negotiation of the Transcontinental Treaty extended the United States to the Pacific Ocean.

As a career diplomat, he helped write the famous Monroe Doctrine in which the United States made it clear that it would not allow any new European colonization in North and South America.

John Quincy and his wife, Louisa, moved into the White House on April 20, 1825. The long delay was due to ongoing health challenges in the life of Mrs. Monroe. The results of these challenges were a series of messy rooms filled with worn rugs, tattered curtains and furniture in the worst of condition. Frustrated by the condition of the White House, especially the presidential living quarters, Louisa Adams not only wrote about it, she went to the extent of inviting people to see how shabby the presidential living quarters were.

Andrew Jackson

Andrew Jackson was a clear example of a poor person reaching the top of American life. He was the first President born in the log cabin of a poor family in South Carolina where his father, Andrew, and his mother, Elizabeth, had moved in 1765. He was born on March 15, 1767, in Waxhaw, South Carolina. He grew up on the poor farm in the frontier of South Carolina.

Two years prior to his birth, Jackson's parents arrived in America from Ireland. A painful experience faced his mother when her husband died just days before her son was born. To further complicate life for Jackson, his mother died when he was fourteen years of age. These experiences left him with little formal education, but his desire to read provided him the opportunity to read the Declaration of Independence aloud before a group of frontier soldiers who could not read. The significance of this is that he was just nine years of age.

Jackson's observation of those frontier soldiers' performance at a revolutionary army crude drilling led him to enlist in the army. He used his ability as an outstanding horseman to enhance his military career by carrying messages from one unit to the next.

During his capture by the British, Jackson was ordered to clean the boots of an English officer. He refused to obey the order, and, as a result, he was struck on the head by the English. The scar on his face was a badge of honor that he wore as a proud American.

Jackson realized that, beyond the battlefield, there was a need to be better prepared. He moved to Salisbury, North Carolina where he studied law and became a practicing lawyer. He went into the deep west to the frontier village of what was known in his days as Nashville. In this trip, he was among the first group of pioneers to travel the Cumberland Trail—the route that most early settlers took to the western territories.

In Nashville, now Tennessee, Jackson was elected General of the people's army against Creek Indians. Though he had very little military training, he was an excellent General who defeated the Creek Indians. This victory promoted him to the rank of General in the federal army. He repeated his success record as a General when he defeated the British in the 1812 war at New Orleans and became a national hero.

Andrew Jackson was the kind of national hero who won the hearts of the American people. He was a man of the people and was the first President who came from humble origins. His personality traits followed him to the very beginning and end of the two terms he served as president. He and Thomas Jefferson shared the tradition of returning to their hotel rooms rather than their official homes on their respective inaugural nights. Jackson also stayed beyond his successor's inaugural and delayed Martin Van Buren's residency.

Jackson was also the first President from the western frontier, and he was very popular with the common people of America. Huge crowds came to Washington D.C. to celebrate his inauguration. They mobbed the White House to shake his hand and wish him well.

Jackson was sent on orders of President James Monroe to put down the uprising by the Seminole Indians living in Spanish-controlled Florida who were carrying out raids across the border of Georgia. The Spanish were protecting the Seminoles. He not only chased the Seminoles into Florida, he attacked and captured the Spanish city of Pensacola. This could have led to war with Spain, but it would have been to the taste of Jackson. However, John Quincy Adams managed to keep the peace.

Jackson in many ways reflected the frontier ideal. He was very combative and confrontational. He was the first President to call himself the elected representative of all the American people. He used the power of the presidency in a very skillful manner. In this light, he vetoed and rejected twelve bills of Congress during his administration. His vetoes became a strategy to make his power and views clear to Congress that the power of the presidency could overrule some of the decisions made by Congress. He is also known to have had a lot of controversial policies such as the rotation in office, the Indian Removal Act and the nullification crisis.

Jackson's philosophy of government was deeply rooted in his understanding that government itself should be plain and simple and that the offices should be rotated among qualified candidates. Even though his opponents called his philosophy the "spoils system" because they held that it was predicated on the military phrase "to the victor goes the spoils," Jackson thought his approach would make government more responsive to the will of the people. Some people felt that by rotating offices, Jackson was doing this to reward his friends and political supporters.

Andrew Jackson's support of the Indian Removal Act of 1830 forced all the Eastern Indian tribes to move to lands west of the Mississippi. By removing the Indians, a lot of valuable land was opened up for the white people. His policy on removal unfairly targeted Indians and caused them untold suffering. In essence, he was justifying that the interest of the white people should be expanded regardless of the devastating consequences to the Indians.

Unlike all other presidents before him, especially George Washington who encouraged a weak presidency, Jackson is said to have ruled as a king. He believed that he had the uncompromising support of the American people. He also felt that leaving the responsibility of lawmaking solely up to Congress undermined the presidency. The President as Chief Executive and Commander-in-Chief, according to Jackson, is to help people get the laws they want and no others. He supported this position by repeatedly vetoing bills passed by Congress and by urging the passage of other bills.

Jackson was swept into the office of President by people from all over the country who believed in his ability to get the job done and felt he was the President of the people. He also ruled as one who felt he had the mandate of the people to epitomize open and simple government to the benefit of all of the people. As indicated earlier, he witnessed people from all over the country gathering to see him take the oath of office, and this probably re-energized his desire to push forward his controversial policies.

Jackson support of a strong presidency, and his sensitivity for the common people reflected his poor background as well as his desire for power. Probably from a modern point of view, Jackson had many faults, but he was a successful politician in his days. He believed in slavery and taught that the only good Indian was a dead Indian or at least one pushed out of white man's territory. But no President except Washington did as much to make the office of the President strong. He was one of the few presidents to finish his second term as popular as when he began his first one.

Jackson believed in limited state rights because he said no one state had the right to decide which national laws it would obey and which it would not. He felt that unlimited state rights would threaten the stability of the Union so vital to all Americans. National laws for Jackson superseded state rights, and he believed they should be enforced at all cost.

Martin
Van Buren

 Martin Van Buren was the son of a Dutch tavern keeper and farmer at Kinderhook, New York. He grew up as a bar boy who sold drinks to New York politicians who stopped at his father's inn while traveling to Albany. By listening to the debates and political intercourse between these politicians, he got an early training in practical politics. He benefited from these politicians and developed a desire for politics at an early age.

Van Buren grew up in a politically charged environment. Voting took place in Kinderhook and so did many legal ideals. Citizens in his hometown discussed politics from different perspectives. Judges and lawyers interacted on cases and matters of concern to a cross section of the town's people. He fell in love with both political and legal aspects of his early environment and decided to use them to his advantage.

Van Buren was the eighth Vice President. He was also the third Vice President to be elected to the office of President. He was the first President to be born after the United States became an independent country. In essence, he was the first United States citizen to become president. He was born a year after the Revolutionary War was won by the Americans, and this made the experiences of all presidents that preceded him different. They were born during the pre-independence era when England still ruled the original colonies, but Van Buren was born at a time when England had absolutely no power over America.

He went to school for a few years at Kinderhook Academy which was a private school in his hometown. At the age of fourteen, he was fortunate to get a job in the law office of Francis Sylvester. His first assignment was to sweep the floors of the office. When he proved himself as a serious and committed worker, he was elevated to a level in the law office where he began to learn about the responsibilities of lawyers. There he learned the theory and actual practice of law.

Van Buren's dedication to the profession of law gave him the opportunity to handle his first case while he was still a teenager. It is believed that he was in court with a lawyer who was arguing a case when suddenly the lawyer turned to Martin and said, "Here, Matt, sum up. You might as well begin early." Although he realized he was unprepared, Van Buren gave it a try. He won the case, and the lawyer paid him a silver half-dollar.

Van Buren's journey in law matured when he became a lawyer at twenty-one years of age. He was, by many accounts, a successful lawyer. His ambition for politics began to surface about this time. He could be likened to a crusader on a mission to realize his passion and interest at all cost.

Van Buren nurtured his political desire by holding some state offices. He became counselor of the New York

Supreme Court and was later appointed by Governor Daniel Tompkins as surrogate of Columbia County. These offices became the foundation for him to foster his greater political desires. He built up a large following by using these offices to give jobs to people who would vote for him and for his political friends. This strategy paid off when he was elected to the United States Senate in 1821 and when he won reelection in 1827.

Van Buren was elected Governor of New York in 1828 and served for only ten weeks before he was appointed by President Jackson to serve as Secretary of State. He used this office to successfully advance his ambition by being Jackson's man. Van Buren realized he did not have the popularity or appeal to become president, so he made himself visible and helpful to President Andrew Jackson during his election. It was this smart move that led Jackson to appoint him Secretary of State. He was a great Secretary of State, and this made him to feel his chances for a greater political future was dependent on his loyalty to President Jackson.

The office of President, which he referred to as "the glittering prize," was getting closer but was yet a long shot away. Van Buren had no doubt he possessed what it took to become president. He was a smart, skillful and articulate politician who had dated politics from an early age and had fallen in love with it. Van Buren had witnessed the interaction of different groups of people in his early years, and he enjoyed doing the same in his adult years. He made his way up the political ladder in such a way that some called him "sly fox."

Van Buren was a man who won the trust of many and proved to be an honest leader. He was willing to use his brilliance to accomplish anything he wanted, but this also created a platform for his critics. Many of his critics felt he was more clever than fair, but President Andrew Jackson strongly supported him and once acknowledged a reference to him as a great magician. President Jackson made it clear that Van Buren's only want was the good common sense he used for the benefit of his country.

In 1832, Martin Van Buren was nominated Vice President by the convention of the newly formed Democratic Party on the ticket headed by Andrew Jackson. They won the election. It is important to note that prior to 1832, the presidential and vice presidential candidates were generally elected by a congressional caucus which consisted of the members of the political parties in Congress.

Van Buren is a clear example of how nicknames can translate into votes and successes. During his bate for the presidency against William Henry Harrison, the voters across the country called him "OK," a nickname for "Old Kinderhook." It played very well with voters who gave him a decisive win. He became President by a 170 to seventy-three electoral vote margin over William H. Harrison.

The reality of the presidency hit home for Van Buren almost as soon as he became President. Delayed in his own residency of the White House by Andrew Jackson, he started an immense campaign of vacating the mansion before a successor's inauguration. This custom has made and continues to make the People's House available on inaugural night to its duly elected occupant. Van Buren's move added a psychological and political balance to the presidency by strategically positioning the President for an immediate start.

Van Buren was faced with a financial crisis known as the "Panic of 1837" that overwhelmed the country. There were failing banks everywhere, and people were suffering great financial loss as the result. Businesses were destroyed, and many people became jobless. The root cause of the problem was gambling. People were borrowing from the bank and investing in markets they thought would bring them greater returns, but the opposite happened.

Van Buren addressed the situation by setting up a separate treasury that would stop another panic from engulfing the nation. He succeeded in helping to develop what we call the U.S. Treasury and the economy got healthy, but his popularity had already suffered an irreversible blow that a favorable trend in job growth could not help. After his 1840 reelection defeat, Van Buren retired to his estate in Lindenwald, Kinderhook. His heart was still committed to the presidency and, in 1848, he became an unsuccessful candidate for President on the Free Soil Party ticket. He died at his Lindenwald estate on July 24, 1862 at age seventy-nine.

William Henry Harrison

 William Henry Harrison returned the office of the President to the Virginia tradition. He was born in Charles City County, Virginia on February 9, 1773 on the family plantation known as Berkeley. His family background had a remarkable history in American political life. His father, Benjamin Harrison, played a significant role in the Revolutionary War and was one of the signers of the Declaration of Independence. He was also Governor of Virginia.

William Henry loved hunting and fishing. Under the leadership of a tutor who taught him all his subjects, he went to grade school until he was fourteen. His college studies started at Hampden-Sydney College in Virginia where he studied classics and history. He went to medical school in Richmond, Virginia and continued it in Philadelphia, Pennsylvania for a short time. His medical studies were designed to satisfy the desire of his father who wanted him to become a medical doctor. He chose to leave his medical studies to become a soldier when his father died in 1791.

At age eighteen, William Henry enlisted as a soldier at Fort Washington, near Wilderness, known today as Cincinnati. He immediately obtained a commission as ensign in the First Infantry Regiment of the regular army and was assigned to the Northwest Territory. This was a frontier region located between the Ohio and Mississippi Rivers. He also became *aide-de-camp* to General "Mad Anthony" Wyne at the Battle of Fallen Timbers. In this position, he was responsible for opening most of the areas in Ohio to the settlers.

During William Henry's seventeen years in the army, he is noted as one who fought in the battle against the Indian tribes in Ohio. He served as General for the American army in the 1812 War and won one of the few United States victories on the border of Canada.

William Henry had a heart and a passion for war. These qualities were manifested when he ably fought against the British army in Michigan and Canada and provided outstanding leadership for the forces that recaptured Detroit from the British army in 1813. Interestingly, he led his armies to victory over the British armies at the battle in Ontario that same year.

At twenty-seven years of age, William Henry was appointed governor of the Indian Territory. He made his way back into the army after serving as Governor. His battle against the Shawnee Indians, known as the Battle of Tippecanoe, earned him the status of a national war hero. The Indians are believed to have attacked the frontier settlements of Indiana. William Henry was entrusted with the task of defending the Territory. He tried all methods to resolve the conflict, but, when in 1809 the outspoken and vital chieftain, Tecumseh, along with his brother, the prophet, rallied the tribes to action, he got permission in

1811 to attack the tribes. When Harrison received permission to attack, he marched with about a thousand men toward the prophet's town. But suddenly, before dawn on November 7 while his small army lay encamped on the Tippecanoe River, the Indians attacked.

There was fierce fighting, but Harrison succeeded in repelling them. One soldier described the bitter encounter in his journal: 190 were dead or wounded in "2 hours and 20 minutes of a continual firing." Harrison went on to destroy the prophet's settlement and proclaim victory. A notable triumph, this was the Battle of Tippecanoe upon which Harrison's future fame was to rest. It disrupted Tecumseh's confederation but failed to diminish the Indian raids which, by the spring of 1812 under British encouragement, terrorized the frontier.

Military life was truly a character and way of life for William Henry. He cherished and loved being a career soldier. His patriotism and interest combined to give him a place in both military and political history. He was a determined man with the guts to support his determination. For example, the Battle at the Tippecanoe River was not considered as a major battle, but it made him famous and gave him the nickname "Old Tippecanoe."

William Henry had a distinguished political life. This provided him the opportunity to serve as Secretary of the Northwest Territory, and he had the confidence of the people in this territory necessary to serve them in the United States Congress. During Harrison's years in Congress, the former Northwest Territory was divided into the Ohio and Indiana territories. These areas were growing because more settlers were moving in. After his term in Congress, Harrison became Governor of Indiana territory covering

Indiana, Michigan, Minnesota, Illinois and Wisconsin. He served as Governor for twelve years.

William Henry's first bit for the presidency as a Whig Party candidate ended in a loss to Martin Van Buren. As a popular candidate, Harrison was again selected by his party to run against Van Buren in very difficult economic and political times. He united the divided Whig Party, rallied the nation to their cause and won the presidency in 1840.

The strategy of the Whig Party was to put forward a noted hero and not necessarily a politician. In this context, William Henry was not a favorite politician, but he was a war hero and that was probably what attracted the Whig Party to him. The Whig Party felt he had what it took to unify the party and win the presidency. The strategy worked, and William Henry Harrison became President of the United States. His family became the first to take residency in the White House on Inauguration Day. His large family of sixteen included extended family members, but it created much confusion and did not become a precedent for some years.

William Henry Harrison was regarded as another Andrew Jackson, and people were excited about him. From his early life, he was either an office holder or an office seeker. His ambition was never hidden from the early days of his life to the time he became President. He was steadfast in seeking what he wanted to accomplish. Harrison died without realizing the extent of his presidential dreams, but his imprint on the presidential map is vivid.

John Tyler

John Tyler was Vice President to William Henry Harrison. He became the first Vice President in the history of the nation to become President upon the President's death. This led to the establishment of a precedent of the Vice President becoming President for the remainder of a term when a president dies in office.

He was born on March 29, 1790 in Charles City County, Virginia. He was the second son John Tyler who was a close friend of Thomas Jefferson and Patrick Henry. His father was a respected judge and Governor of Virginia. He and Harrison were sons of Virginian governors. He went to college when he was just twelve years old and, considering his mother died when he was seven years old, he was a good and exceptional student. When he graduated from college, he studied law under his father and was admitted to the bar in 1809.

John's belief in the rights of the states and his commitment to the limited power of the federal government became both his strength and weakness in politics. In 1827 he was elected to the United States Senate and was reelected in 1833 where he manifested a strong support for state rights and openly spoke his mind on the issues of the day. He resigned his seat in the Senate as a protest to the Virginia Legislative Delegation that tried to tell him how he should vote.

It is believed that John resisted strict discipline and was a radical from the early days of his life. John attended a local school in Charles City County where he was an excellent student. It is also believed that, when he was ten, he led a classroom revolt against the teacher, Mr. McMurdoo. This revolt took place because John and his classmates thought Mr. McMurdoo was too strict. John and some of his classmates tied him up and left him in the classroom, but a passerby who heard his cries for help rescued him. After being freed by the passerby, Mr. McMurdoo complained to Tyler's father. He hoped he would punish his son for leading the revolt. John's father did not punish him. Instead, as a judge, he reminded the angry teacher of Virginia's state motto: *Sic Semper Tyrannis* (Thus Always to Tyrants). The act of opposing his unpopular schoolmaster helped Tyler display a sense of independence which characterized his life in politics.

Tyler became Vice President because the Whig Party wanted some one to create a balance to the presidential ticket. He was from the south and the votes of the south were crucial to a Harrison win. The party knew Harrison was known through the country as a man from the West, and without a balance to attract southerners, a Whig victory would be impossible. Tyler was the right man at the right time. His family had name recognition, and he had graduated from William and Mary at the age of seventeen. He became a member of the Virginia Legislature at twenty-one. He was a member of the House of Representatives from Virginia and Governor of Virginia. He also became a United States Senator for Virginia. However, his popularity was limited to his home state.

The dream of John ever becoming President of the United States was the remotest thing from the imagination of his party. He was not regarded as presidential material. The idea of a Vice President becoming President was alien to the political landscape of the country.

Tyler's presidency opened the eyes of the nation to the possibility that a president was subject to death like everyone else. It also taught the nation to look at the office of Vice President beyond the role of ticket balance. The Vice President was no longer regarded as a ceremonial figure but as a possible successor to the President of the United States. He was left with limited powers, and this affected his ability to function as President, but his future prospects were no longer taken for granted.

Tyler was a political revolutionary who held to his beliefs for most of his political life. His record in Congress clearly shows his values. Like his father's friend, Thomas Jefferson, he thought the federal government should keep out of the states' business. Tyler had always voted against spending federal money for such things as roads and harbors. He had originally been a Democrat, not a Whig, and had supported Andrew Jackson for President. He changed party in opposition to Jackson who claimed too much power for the federal government. He turned against Jackson and members of Democratic Party and joined the Whig Party. It was largely because of this that he was regarded as a Whig, although none of his ideas had changed. He still believed strongly in states' rights.

In 1840 Tyler was unanimously nominated by the Whig Party as its vice presidential candidate on the ticket headed by the war hero, General William Henry Jackson. Using the campaign slogan, "Tippecanoe and Tyler too," Harrison and Tyler easily won the election but, on April 4, 1841, a month after Harrison became president, he died in office. Tyler was informed of Harrison's death while he was at home in Williamsburg, Virginia and immediately returned to Washington, D.C. He was able to transcend all questions and doubts regarding his actual position. Many people did not know if he was the new President or if he was the Vice President. By taking the Presidential Oath and assuming all the powers and duties of the President, Tyler made a statement as President.

In the minds of the party's leaders, Tyler was nothing more than a caretaker President. They wanted the party to tell Tyler how to govern the nation, but they were in for a great surprise. The Whigs thought Tyler would take his marching orders from their leadership or from Harrison's Cabinet without any changes. They underestimated Tyler's knowledge of the presidency. He knew he was leader of the party, but they did not see it that way.

When Harrison became President, he apparently agreed to let the majority of his Cabinet make the crucial decisions. Daniel Webster, Secretary of State, shared information with Tyler hoping he would conform to the decisions of President Harrison, but Tyler remained independent. His independent policies made the Whigs want to expel him from the party in September 1841. This put him in an awkward position. He was a President who enjoyed no party loyalty because he had no party support for the rest of his term. To complicate matters, his wife died during this period, but in less than two years after his first wife's death, he married Julia Gardiner of New York and they had five sons and two daughters. Tyler became the first President to marry while in office.

When he became President, Tyler took the bold steps of reorganizing the Navy and establishing the Weather Bureau. He opened the Orient to American trade, ended the Seminole War and approved statehood for Florida and Texas. He was a man of unwavering conviction, not afraid to take risks for what he believed was right. His life after the presidency was active and practical. He retired to his estate in Virginia where he continued the practice of law and actively participated in public affairs.

When he died on January 18, 1862, his death was totally ignored by the government; but in 1911, Congress authorized the erection of a monument to his memory in Hollywood Cemetery, Richmond, Virginia. The government's attitude at the time was predicated upon the active role he played during the Civil War. When the Civil War broke up in 1861, Tyler tried very hard to prevent secession, but he later gave up all hope of establishing peace and supported his state's secession from the Union. He was elected to the Confederate (Southern) House of Representatives in November of 1861, but he died before the legislative body met.

James K. Polk

James Knox Polk was a horse racer, and his boyhood friends called him "Black Pony" due to his passion for this sport. It was not a racist statement but a social joke. He grew up on his family farm, the first of the ten children of Samuel and Jane Knox Polk. He was the great-grand nephew of the highly noted Presbyterian reformer John Knox.

James Polk learned to read and write at home because he was too sickly to go to school. When he was ten, his family moved to Tennessee where he grew up.

His early health difficulties were helped when he was about sixteen and his doctor discovered he was suffering from a gallstone, a painful stone-like object that can form in the gallbladder. James survived this dangerous condition at age seventeen when he successfully overcame a risky and painful operation. It was a complex situation as doctors did not yet have anaesthetic. After this experience, he became a healthy and energetic youth who followed his dream for higher education. His serious nature was demonstrated in his early school records which indicated he never missed a class or failed to do his homework. Polk was a person of commitment and vision who worked to see his dream come true. His successful recovery led him to the University of North Carolina where he graduated in 1818 with honors in mathematics and the classics.

In 1820, James Polk became a practicing lawyer after studying law with a lawyer named Felix Grundy in Nashville, Tennessee. During his law studies he developed an interest in politics and joined the Democratic Party. He was a friend and supporter of Andrew Jackson who was Governor of Tennessee at the time he was elected to the State Legislature in 1823. Polk and Jackson had differences in their personalities. Polk was a quiet, formal and hard-working man with slender build, gray eyes and long hair hanging over his neck. Andrew Jackson was colorful, out-spoken and always ready for a fight. But Polk and Jackson believed in the phrase used by those who held the conviction that the United States should expand all the way to the Pacific Ocean: "manifest destiny."

James Polk fought for the common people and defended them against economic injustices. This fight was manifested in his opposition to the powerful speculators and bankers whose interest he taught directly contradicted those of the common people. He was a serious lawmaker whose commitment to hard work on congressional business elevated him to a position of prominence among his fellow representatives. In 1835, he was chosen as Speaker of the House of Representatives. His effective service as head of the body responsible for writing tax laws, the Ways and Means Committee, won the hearts of his fellow legislators.

James Polk is known in United States presidential politics as the first "dark-horse" President because it was believed he would be unable to win the presidency but he proved the critics wrong and won the election. He defeated Henry Clay, who had fame and name recognition, because he took the bold step of declaring himself for the taxes annexation.

James Polk had a distinguished service record in United States political life, but not many people, especially his critics, believed he would be able to win the presidency. He was the first Speaker of the House of Representatives to become President of the United States. As the man who ran the House of Representatives, he was the third most powerful person of the United States government. He was a Congressman for fourteen years and a crucial player in both Andrew Jackson's presidential victory in 1828 and ensuring that President Jackson's policies were accepted by the House of Representatives.

Mr. Polk had a good record of service and a workable strategy to support President Jackson, but they were not enough for the kind of national appeal needed to become President of the United States. It took his home district to elect him to Congress and his peers in Congress to elect him as Speaker of the House, and it would take a nationwide appeal to make him a major presidential contender.

Initially, Mr. Polk was not in the lineup for president. The two major players in putting him there were former President Martin Van Buren and Mr. Lewis Cass. When it became clear that neither of the two could win the majority of the party's votes at the Democratic Convention, James Polk, candidate for Vice President, was elected. It was a political battle, but he won on the ninth ballot. The party leadership trusted him, and the delegates voted for him because they believed he could win the White House for them.

James Polk was no stranger to the political reality of life. His successes were as helpful as his failures in politics. When he left Congress, he retired on his farm for a short period, and that same year, he ran for and won the election for Governor. He served for a period of two years. However, his bid for the same position in 1841 and 1843 showed different results. He was acquainted with the political balance and compromise needed for a career in politics.

James Polk supported his mentor Andrew Jackson who was known as "Old Hickory." He used that support to his advantage when he ran as "Young Hickory." Texas was a major political issue because it was an independent country that had just broken away from Mexico. Henry Clay, who was running against James Polk, was vigorously against any immediate action to annex Texas to the United States. James Polk was elected because he skillfully supported expansion of the United States territories. He chose the Texas issue, popular with the southern voters, and the question of Oregon popular with the North.

James Polk enjoyed the support of Andrew Jackson. Jackson devoted himself to the support Polk's campaign, and used his political experience to draw a crucial conclusion for Polk. He determined that most of the electorate accepted territorial expansion because it was vital to national security. Jackson believed that Polk was the candidate committed to the nation's "manifest destiny," and he wrote letters urging people to support his friend. Jackson responded to the Whigs' mockery question, "Who is James Polk?" by publishing an extensive letter which stated: "His capacity for business is great... and to extraordinary powers of labor, both mental and physical, he unites that tact and judgment which are requisite to the successful direction to such an office."

James Polk shared his four-point platform with historian George Bancroft shortly after his inauguration. He told Bancroft he wanted the reduction of the tariff, the independent treasury, the settlement of the Oregon boundary question and the acquisition of California. With the support of his Cabinet and Democratic Congressional friends, President Polk succeeded in accomplishing all of his goals.

In 1846, the Walker Tariff Act, taxes on import and the Independent Treasury Act passed by Congress became law. Congress made the division on the other two goals before Polk became President. It passed a joint resolution offering annexation to Texas before Polk became President as a way of avoiding war with Mexico. To avoid war with the British, President Polk settled the issue of Oregon that extended to the Canadian boundary.

Polk distinguished himself as a very hard-working President who was one of the strongest and most successful presidents of the nineteenth century. Under his leadership, Congress passed laws that restored an important treasury and reduced tariffs on imports. His greatest achievement was the expansion of American control in the west. The dispute over the Texas border led to the Mexican War in 1846. At the completion of the War in 1848, the U.S. gained California, Utah and New Mexico territories. Polk also settled the border between the Oregon territory and Canada.

James Polk wanted to be a one-term President to avoid distraction from his worth as President. He put the greater good of his country before the politics of re-election. When he left the presidency, he returned home to Nashville, Tennessee with his wife. His commitment to duty and his hard work left him in poor health when he retired from the presidency. Just three months after he left, he fell ill and died on June 15, 1849 at the age of fifty-four.

Zachary Taylor

 Zachary Taylor was the product of military life, and he grew up with stories of drilling and fighting. His father was an officer in the Revolutionary War. Former President James Madison and General Robert E. Lee were his cousins. He was born on November 24, 1784 in Orange County, Virginia. Zachary's father, Richard, fought in the Revolutionary War with George Washington. He was rooted in Virginian life, but he was raised in the small frontier village of Louisville, Kentucky.

Zachary learned how to read and write at home because his services were needed on the family farm. He had very little formal education and spent most of his youthful days working on the farm. Zachary later joined the army as a private, and two years later, he became a lieutenant. He was committed to the life and blood of the United States and did all he could to make his country prevail over its enemies.

Zachary was nicknamed "Old Rough and Ready" because he was always ready to hold the Union together by armed force rather than to promote a compromise. It is interesting to note that Zachary Taylor's background would have made him a supporter of the south, but he did all he could to keep the Union together and alive.

Zachary Taylor was a small man in stature but a great man in action. He was a slave owner, but he was also far ahead of his time on the issue of slavery. Frank Freidel writes that being a slaveholder did not make Taylor a defender of slavery or of southern sectionalism. His forty years in the army had imbued him with a strong nationalist spirit. He received a commission in the regular army in 1808 and spent decades policing the frontier against Indians, especially during the War of 1812.

Taylor was assigned to the Indiana territory during the Black Hawk War. He was also assigned to Florida during the long struggle of the Seminole Indians. Taylor won victories at Monterrey and Buena Vista during the Mexican War because he used much of the same direct offensive tactics he had employed against the Indians.

Taylor fought against Chief Black Hawk and against the Seminoles in Florida. He was made General during the Seminoles War. When Texas became a part of the United States in 1845, most of the people thought the Nuccees River was actually the border of Texas. However, President Polk invoked the Mexican War by sending General Taylor with an army beyond the Nuccees River to the Rio Grande. The struggle for power transcended all principles of democracy and employed the age-old military expression, "Might makes right."

Zachary Taylor was not regarded as an outstanding General in the early stages of his career. His fame as General and war hero came during the Battle of Buena Vista. He defeated Mexican armed forces four times the size of the one he was commanding. Succeeding over the enemies made him a national hero and a public figure.

Millard Fillmore

Millard Fillmore was the son of a farmer and the second of nine children. His family was very poor, and he began working on the farm at an early age. Plowing, hoeing corn, mowing hay and harvesting wheat were some of the basic skills he learned as a farm helper. His responsibilities on the farm made him irregular at the one-room house he attended school. The formal education he received came from his own efforts and determination. The family farm was a small one located near the Finger Lakes of New York State. It was only a way of survival and not much more than a clearing hacked out of the woods on the frontier.

Millard's father thought his son should learn trade under a person experienced in the art. He felt this would better his son's life. He sent him away at age fifteen to learn trade and, in the process, he worked to take care of his room and food. When he became President years later, he was nicknamed the "Wool-Carder President" because he worked in a cloth-making factory when he was younger.

Millard Fillmore had greater ambition than working as a wool-carder running machines that spun wool into yarn. During his free time, he attended an academy in New Hope, New York. He was an out-of-place eighteen-year-old in class with children who were seven and eight. He was a handsome and tall young man. His teacher was a fine red-haired young lady named Abigail Powers. She was the daughter of Reverend Lemuel Powers of Moravia, and she later became Millard's wife. Abigail invested much time and effort in teaching Millard. As a result, he developed enough confidence to move beyond his present environment. He fell in love with Abigail, but their wedding did not take place until later in life because Millard wanted to be in a position to support his family.

When Millard completed his training as a wool-carder, he went on to become a clerk for Judge Walter Wood in Montville, New York in whose office he started reading law at age eighteen. He was motivated to study law, and he also taught school to maintain himself. In 1823, he became a practicing lawyer after he was admitted to the bar, and he went on to open his own law office in East Aurora, near Buffalo. In 1830, he relocated his law practice to New York. On February 5, 1826, he married Abigail; they had two children, a son and a daughter.

Millard Fillmore became a successful lawyer in New York where he also became active in politics. He served in the New York State Assembly and was later elected to Congress as a member of the Whig Party. This was partly because of his connection with Thurlow Weed, but he proved himself one who appreciated the opportunity to serve. During his terms in Congress, from 1836 to 1844, he supported high tariffs on imports and stood firmly against citizenship for new immigrants. He became one of the leaders for the Whig Party and, between 1841 and 1843, served as Chairman of the Ways and Means Committee.

Millard Fillmore's first run for office was in 1828 for the New York State Legislature, and he served in this capacity for three terms. His greatest accomplishment in this position was to end the practice of imprisoning people who were in debt. When he returned to New York and was serving his state as Comptroller, he became one of the greatest contributing factors in improving the state's banking system. He knew what was needed for the state because he had run an unsuccessful campaign to be Governor of New York prior to becoming Comptroller.

In 1848, he was elected to serve as Vice President by the National Convention of the Whig Party on the ticket headed by General Zachary Taylor. Unlike presidential races today in which the President interviews and makes the ultimate decision on who will be his running mate, the Party made the choice in Fillmore's day. So, when Millard Fillmore was nominated as Vice President to Zachary Taylor, both men didn't know each other as they had never met prior to being narrowly elected.

In the office of Vice President, Fillmore presided over the Senate during the months of nerve-wracking debate over the Compromise of 1850. Fillmore looked more the part of President than Taylor. He was a very tall, handsome, impeccably groomed, good-natured man who labored to maintain an atmosphere of fairness in the Senate Chamber. There was no public comment on the merits of the compromise proposals by the Vice President. A few days before President Taylor's death, Fillmore intimated to him that if there should be a tie vote on Clay's bill in the Senate, he would vote in favor of it.

Fillmore was highly regarded by the people in the State of Utah. They named their capital city in his honor with the hopes he would grant them statehood. When he failed to do so, the capital was later changed from Fillmore to Salt Lake. Utah and Salt Lake City have become the focus of the world's attention because they hosted the 2002 Winter Olympics. In an historic move, the Secret Service took over security at the Olympic games because of continuous fear of terrorist threats. It is fair to note that the Olympics was as controversial as the history of its host city. Utah and Salt Lake played great hosts to the Olympic games, and it was recorded as a great success.

Fillmore probably would have regretted his decision not to grant Utah statehood. In retrospect, he would have listened to the people of Utah and granted their wishes, but he still would have played politics to the very end.

Franklin Pierce

 Franklin Pierce was the first President born in the nineteenth century. He became President during a period of relative peace, but the country was still divided on ideological grounds. The issues of the past were stormy, and they made domestic policies difficult for this young and inexperienced President. There were vast differences between the North, who was opposed to slavery, and the South, who supported it. This made him indecisive and, to some extent, an ineffective President.

When Franklin Pierce became President, he pleased the Southern planters by proclaiming that anti-slavery agitation must be condemned and that the tariff should be lowered. His position on slavery led to a national crisis and cost him the loss of his presidency to James Buchanan. The Democrats were upset with Pierce, and they were looking for a candidate who was not clear-cut and resolute on "Southern principles." They soon discovered that James Buchanan of Pennsylvania was the right man at the right time. His victory was responsible for sending Pierce back to the green hills of New Hampshire. He returned home, broken-hearted and probably destroyed.

Franklin Pierce was born into a family known for its deep commitment to military and political services. Both his father and oldest brother fought in the Revolutionary War and the War of 1812. His father, Benjamin, had been a General in the Revolutionary War, and he later became Governor of New Hampshire. When his father became Governor in 1827, Franklin's interest in politics was ignited. His original desire was to become a soldier, but he changed his mind and decided to seek the path of politics.

Pierce graduated from Bowdoin College, Maine in 1827 where he studied Greek, Latin, science and math. He focused his attention on the study of law and later became a lawyer. In 1829, he ran for the New Hampshire Congress where he served for four years, and in 1833, he ran for the House of Representatives and served for four years. He won the election for the United States Senate and became the youngest person in the Senate during his time of service. He was educated in the business of politics.

The two Generals, Winfield Scott and Franklin Pierce, were offered to the people in 1852 for their consideration. Scott represented the Whigs, and Pierce represented the Democrats. Pierce was the lesser star in military firmament. He had fought in the war against Mexico and been injured when he was thrown off his horse on the battlefield. Pierce gained great appreciation for his services and sacrifices. He was no match to the distinguished record of General Winfield Scott. Pierce had, on the other hand, proven to be a better politician than Scott. He knew how to adapt and how to negotiate.

Franklin Pierce was a dark horse in the national field because his national popularity was limited. His party, the Democrats, did not select him until the forty-ninth ballot. He appealed to a cross section of society because of his open nature and approach. For example, he was considered a "Northern man with Southern principles," and that gave him support from the South. He was a champion of religious liberty, and that won him the favor of the Irish members of Tammany Hall. His campaign biography written by his friend, Nathaniel Hawthorne, climaxed it all. In return for his pains and efforts, Pierce rewarded him with an office.

Franklin Pierce encountered lots of trials and tribulations in his journey of life. In 1853, two months after he was elected President, his eleven-year old son, Benny, was killed in a train accident. The death of their only surviving child caused Jane, his wife, to detest moving to Washington. She was so deeply grieved, it took two months after her husband's inauguration for her to come to Washington. In the White House, his wife did not seek support for her grief. This made her bear it alone and added a sad chapter to their lives. His aunt, Abby Kent Means, stepped in and became the hostess for the White House during the Pierce presidency.

James Buchanan

James Buchanan never married. He stayed single because of disappointment and frustration. His sweetheart, Ann Coleman, who he met while serving in the legislature, broke up their relationship. They both loved each other, but her father, who was a wealthy Pennsylvania businessman, felt James only wanted his daughter because she was rich. Her parents forced her to break their 1819 engagement and her relationship with James. Shortly after the breakup, Ann got sick and died, and this sad chapter in his life led him to make a vow he would never marry.

When Buchanan became President, the issue of slavery had become the dominating factor in American politics. There were violent protests and many disagreements over slavery being allowed in the newly expanded areas. The people of the Northern states, who were opposed to slavery, held the view that Buchanan was pro-slavery. The people from the Southern states, who supported slavery in all the newly expanded areas, threatened to leave the Union because of the slavery issue. Buchanan's desire to save the Union led him to push for a compromise between the North and South. He was opposed to slavery, but he felt that saving the Union was his primary and civic responsibility.

The conflict between his morality and civic responsibility became more challenging when the Supreme Court made one of its most famous and controversial decisions—the Dred Scott decision—during his first week as President. Mr. Scott was a slave who had been taken to a non-slave area where he demanded he be treated as a free man. He saw his residence in a free area as a just reason to be treated as free. He took his demand to court because he learned that the United States Congress had passed a law that slavery should not exist in free territory. The Supreme Court ruled that the Congress had no right to pass a law limiting slavery.

Abraham Lincoln

Abraham Lincoln was born in a log cabin built by his father, Thomas, a farmer. His only brother, Thomas, died in infancy. Abraham grew up with his father, his mother, Nancy, and sister, Sarah. He was born on February 12, 1809 in Hardin County, Kentucky. Both children put in long hours of work on the farm, but at eight years of age, his family relocated to Indiana. His father was regarded as a ne'er-do-well farmer who drifted from one place to another along the frontier.

Lincoln was afraid of war and had strong feelings about it. His father had shared the story concerning the death of his father. It is believed that Lincoln's grandfather, Abraham, was shot by an Indian in an incident that took place in the presence of his son. Lincoln's Uncle Mord shared the same story, but in him it didn't create any bad feelings toward Indians or Black people. He knew the history of the country and could see the bad treatment Indians and Black people had suffered at the hand of White men.

The Indians, in some situations, were wrong for pro-voking and attacking white people, but Lincoln felt this didn't merit the mass murder of their people. He also knew that Black people were wrong in some instances when they led fatal rebellions against the Whites, but he did not feel this was adequate to continue the acts of slavery.

Lincoln was opposed to slavery as much as he was opposed to the oppression of Indians. Here was a white man who risked his present, future and transcended his pain of the past to advocate for settlers and for slaves. He had an inclusive view of humanity, and he did all he could to ensure the greater good of all people and, above all, a wholesome future for his country.

When he saved the life of an Indian who was about to be killed by Lincoln's own troops, he pleaded mercy and forgiveness. He knew the danger, but he lived in the belief that a life truly controlled by God must respect the lives of others. This man volunteered his life and services at an early age. He served the good of his country and the betterment of all his people. When the War days were over, young Lin-coln was happy for two reasons: he had served his country well, and he didn't have to shoot anyone.

Abraham Lincoln was nicknamed "the Rail-Splitter" because he proved to be a great ax user. He had used the ax to split logs for his cabin and for fences. His hard teamwork with his father was manifested in the services he shared clearing the land and building a cabin on their new property in Indiana. He is believed to have made this remark about his schooling: "There were some schools, so called, but they all taught us readin', writin', and cipherin'."

When Lincoln matured enough to make his own deci-sions, he developed interest in reading and used all the resources around him to become one of the best readers of history. He spent nights reading by the light of an open fire.

Lincoln was a gifted storyteller and public speaker. During his boyhood, he told stories that made people laugh, and he was greatly admired for his gift. People who trusted and believed in him transcended the heroic aspects of his life and dwelled on the importance of the individual himself.

Abraham Lincoln was a person who experienced failure firsthand. He tried jobs on a flatboat going to New Orleans, in a country store and as a surveyor. He knew what it was to be poor and struggling. When the office of President afforded him the opportunity to make a difference, he changed the American political landscape. He often took the side of the socially and politically oppressed. Lincoln knew what things looked like from the other side of the social and political ladder. He longed to make a change provided the opportunity availed itself.

Lincoln was married to Mary Todd, and they had four sons, but three of them died before reaching adulthood. Edward died at age four, William at age eleven and Thomas at eighteen. These events made life very difficult for the Lincolns, but their son, Robert, provided hope for his parents. He was a distinguished statesman and Secretary of War for President James Garfield.

When Lincoln became President, there were more difficulties than anticipated. The Democratic Party that elected him split into two parts prior to his presidency. One part supported the principles and ideologies of the South, and the other part supported the principles and ideologies of the North. He wanted to save the Union through a skillful approach that included all people, and he employed all methodologies to get his aim accomplished.

Lincoln won the election in the fall of 1860, but he did not take office until March 1861. During this period, one Southern state after another voted to leave the Union and establish a new government. Frustrated by the process and confusion, President James Buchanan decided to let them have their wish. Lincoln was moving into dangerous territory, but he realized that the power of the presidency provided a unique opportunity for the President to lead the nation through challenging times.

After Lincoln took the Oath of the President of the United States on March 4, 1861, he did not take any action until a month had passed. He probably knew he was confronted by circumstances beyond his control, but he also recognized the power of the office that was laid at his heart and hands. Lincoln did not want to provoke the boarder states that were undecided about their commitment to stay in the Union. The strategy he developed to please those in the North who did not believe in the Union nor that the issue of slavery warranted a fight was received with mixed feelings. President Lincoln wanted a fight on the grounds that he would gain support for the War on all fronts, but he was resolute about the stability of the Union.

The Lincoln administration was forced into war on April 12, 1861 when Southern troops fired on the Lincoln-held Fort Sumter in Charleston, South Carolina. Lincoln feasted on the patriotism of the North and used its support to his advantage. He used this war experience to advance himself during the next four years of his presidency. These were very difficult days in the life of the country, but Lincoln won the battle as a great President.

Lincoln was a lawyer who was later elected to the State Legislature and to the United States Congress from Illinois.

He stood against slavery as a Congressman and proposed a law that the government should buy all slaves in the District of Columbia and set them free. His law did not pass, but his conviction that slavery was wrong could not be removed. After returning to Illinois with his family, Lincoln was elected to the United States Senate by his state because he was seen to have been the right person to deal with the prevailing circumstances hunting the nation.

Lincoln became the champion of the new Republican Party and a true ambassador for a free society. The new Party was able to attract many Whig Party members to its causes. The fight against slavery and the broad based economic program of the new Republican Party won over members of the old party and independent voters. To the exclusion of slavery from the territories, it added an endorsement of the protective tariff and of the long-debated project for giving away public lands as homesteads to farmers and laborers.

It was made clear that, in states where slavery existed, the labor system was not to be disturbed but it was to be excluded from the territories of the Great West. When the platform with these elements was read at the Republican convention in 1860, the free-soil plank was applauded. When the tariff and homestead clauses were presented, the people greeted them with outstanding and prolonged cheers.

Abraham Lincoln did not get along with his own Cabinet. His style of governance was alien to some of them. They did not understand him or his leadership style. He looked like a tall man who had bought his clothes second-hand from a person four inches shorter than he was, but he was resolute in his conviction to make a difference on the slavery issue.

The four years that followed were probably the most desperate in the history of the United States. In these years, Lincoln proved himself to be a great President, but his humanity led him to make some mistakes. He probably did not do enough to understand the people around him. There were two things that resulted from the misunderstanding between Lincoln and the people he had invited to serve with him. He tried one General after another before he found a really good one. He did not get alone with his own Cabinet.

Lincoln built a reputation as a ruthless leader who treated people like pieces of wood. He was task oriented. He was also a leader who wanted to see the job done. In other words, he was a person who held the philosophy of "work before play."

Lincoln was not totally new to politics. He had some experience. He served three terms as State Legislator for Illinois. In this position, he proved himself effective and charming as a politician. Lincoln was not a professional politician, but he was drawn into politics because of his dislike for manual labor.

Lincoln was honest, faithful, friendly and an outstanding storyteller who won the hearts of the people in his state. In the State Legislature, he was known for his ability to form coalitions and win over others to the platform of his Party. He knew how to keep secrets, how to trade favors, how to get the attention of the higher-ups in the Whig Party and how to use the Press in his favor.

Lincoln was elected to Congress as a member of the Minority Whig Party in 1846 and a junior Congressman from Illinois. In this position, he did not win much national distinction and became unpopular in his own home state for opposing President Polk for his stance on the Mexican War.

The frustration in Washington and the dejection back home made him return to his thriving law practice after a single term in Congress.

Lincoln in many ways demonstrated both his emotions and skills for what he taught was right and just for all people. He was unlike Stephen A. Douglas, his Democratic rival. Lincoln was committed to fighting for all people, including the common people. The difference between Lincoln and Douglas was soon to draw national and international attention. It would become a historic landmark and an academic stimulation for people in all areas of life.

Lincoln said that the repeal of the Missouri Compromise aroused him as he had never been before. The Mis-Compromise had drawn a line to exclusively keep slavery in the South. The repeal give the green light for slavery to spread into Kansas, Nebraska and throughout the West. This was both a major victory for slave owners and an expansion of the slave industry to other territories. It also meant that dismantling slavery would definitely amount to dissolving the Union.

The Missouri Compromise presented a life that was complicated and confusing to Lincoln and those who shared his strong conviction against slavery. Unlike all other experiences, this event became the turning point in Lincoln's life, and it moved him into greater action against slavery. He again developed interest in politics because he regarded the Missouri Compromise and repeal as a covert deal he could not accept. It had the face of compromise, but the deeper root was to continue slavery indefinitely.

The showdown against the Missouri Compromise actually began in 1858, after Lincoln had joined the newly formed Republican Party and was recognized as the right person to oppose Douglas for a seat in the Senate. Prior to that time, he had made lots of anti-slavery speeches setting the stage for an all-out fight against the Compromise.

He delivered speeches of inclusion, and Abraham Lincoln opened his campaign for the Senate with his moving "House Divided" speech. He said: "I believe this government can not endure, permanently half slave and half free. I do not expect the Union to be dissolved—I do not expect the house to fall—but I do expect it will cease to be divided. It will become all one thing, or all another." In a series of debates, he challenged Douglas' teaching of popular sovereignty and classified it as a policy that was a direct contradiction to the question of right and wrong.

Lincoln felt that Douglas was for slavery, a position he regarded as a moral, social and political evil. "Let us have faith that right makes might and in that faith, let us, to the end, dare to do our duty as we understand it." He ordered the transcripts from the debates to be published. When the book was finally published, it became a best seller. His following and popularity increased dramatically. He was now a national figure with his eyes on the greater prize—the presidency. A public relations campaign was immediately started, and Lincoln went to New York to market himself.

The result of the election was a sad commentary on the ethical, moral, social and political life of America. Douglas won that election for the Senate, but Lincoln's stance against institutionalized racism, his call for a free and just society eventually took him to the White House. In 1856, Lincoln joined the Republican Party because he agreed with the principle the Party was created upon in 1854. The founders of the Republican Party were people who were opposed to slavery in the new territories and probably to institutionalized slavery as well.

Lincoln became the most strategic choice for presidential candidate because he could appeal to voters in the old stronghold of Jacksonian Democracy. He was the son of a poor farmer with historical ties to the Kentucky, Indiana and Illinois tradition of hard work in field and forest. As a member of the humble tradition of the log cabin, which had been used with great effect in many campaigns, he was remotely associated to the culture of rich Whigs and rich planters.

Since Andrew Jackson, all politicians had paid tribute to the log cabin people. Lincoln had been there. He had hoed corn, split rails, boated on the Mississippi, kept a general store, practiced law on the frontier, told stories and joked with hunters, farmers and day laborers. He had graduated from the college of hard knocks and was adequately prepared to face the challenges of life hunting the Union. Lincoln was often overlooked, but he was a fighter for his country and for all of the people.

It is believed that there was little in Lincoln's background and appearance to inspire confidence that he could meet the challenge posed by the tier of states in the deep South that had seceded to form the Confederacy. Some reporters traveling eastward with the newly elected President remembered how dismayed people were by Lincoln's high-pitched voice. They noticed how people regarded him as an individual with awkward manners. But these superficialities were quickly overshadowed as the true nature of Lincoln was seen when he began to take action as President.

Lincoln transcended mere appearance and impression, but he never lived beyond his conviction that slavery was wrong. He was committed to the greater good of his country. He wanted a United States predicated on the basic principles of freedom, justice, equality and fair play. Lincoln's position on the slavery issue was voiced even when he was in the United States Congress. He stood on his principles of inclusion.

He came from a humble and hard-working background. The joking phrase "Abe Lincoln, the rail splitter" became the rallying cry during his run for presidency. Throughout his campaign, he was hailed as an honest, humorous and friendly man who stood for the rights of all. The campaign played down his high-profile career as a lawyer.

He built for himself a reputation as a great man, a unique President and an outstanding statesman. Lincoln was the people's President at a time when America was too divided to embrace his inclusive leadership. He did not permit the institution of the Executive to destroy his will and passion to stand for unpopular ideas.

Lincoln knew that a great and kind America should be an inclusive nation where the voices of all people were heard and respected. Lincoln's America is the America we are seeking to achieve today, but to do this, we have to face the reality that we are all in the process of becoming the colorful nation we are intended to be.

Endnotes

1. p. 15. Pious, Richard, M, *The Young Oxford Companion to the Presidency of the United States*, Oxford University Press Inc.: New York, 1993, p.270.

2. p. 23. Beschloss, Michael, *American Heritage*, New York: American Heritage, Inc., 2000, p. 35.

3. p.26. Harris, Laurie Lanzen, *Biography for Beginners, Presidents of the United States*, Michigan: Favorable Impression, Omnigraphics, Inc., 1998, p.21.

4. p.34. Mapp, Jr., Alf J, *Thomas Jefferson: Passionate Pilgrim*, Lanham, Maryland: Madison Books, 1991, p.264.

5. p.35. Severance, John B, *Thomas Jefferson, Architect of Democracy*, New York: Clarion Books, 1998, p. 56-67.

6. p.40. Garraty, John A., *1001 Things Everyone Should*

Know About American History, New York: Doubleday. 1989, p.24.

7. p. 48. Blassingame, Wyatt, *The Look-It-Up Book of Presidents*, New York: Random House, 2001, p.29.

8. p.48. Ibid., 29.

9. p.48. Ibid., 29.

10. p.56. Harris, Laurie Lanzen, *Biography for Beginners*, p.69.

11. p.63. Beard, Charles, A., *The Presidents in American History*, Cambridge: Julian Messner, 1989, p.38.

12. p.69. Beschloss, Michael, *American Heritage*, p. 29.

13. p.80-81. Harris, Laurie Lanzen, *Biography for Beginners*, p.104.

14. p. 98. Blassingame, Wyatt. *The Look-It-Up Book of Presidents*, p.58.

15. p.104. Burchard, Peter, *Lincoln and Slavery*, New York: Atheneum Books for Young Readers, 1999, p.53.

Bibliography

Anthony, Carl Sferrazza. *America's First Families*. New York: Simon & Schuster, 2000.

Beard, Charles A. *The Presidents in American History*. Cambridge: Julian Messner, 1989.

Beschloss, Michael. *American Heritage*. New York: American Heritage Inc., 2000.

Bober, Natalie S. *Abigail Adams*. New York: Atheneum Books for Young Readers, 1995.

Boller, Jr., Paul F. *Presidential Inaugurations*. New York: Harcourt INC., 2001.

Bowen, Catherine Brinker. *John Adams*. Boston: Little, Brown and Company, 1858.

Burchard, Peter. *Lincoln and Slavery*. New York: Atheneum Books for Young Readers, 1999.

Cunliffe, Marcus. *George Washington*. New York: American Heritage Publishing Co., Inc., 1966.

Dole, Bob. *Great Presidential Wit*. New York: Scribner, 2001.

Doris Faber and Harold Faber. *Great Lives*. New York: Atheneum Books for Young Readers, 1988.

Feerick, John D. and Emalie P. *The First Book of Vice-Presidents*. New York/London: Franklin Watts Inc., 1961.

Fleming, Thomas J. *First in Their Hearts*. New York: Walker Publishing Company, Inc., 1985.

Guelzo, Allen C. *Abraham Lincoln*. Michigan: Wm. B. Eerdmans Publishing Co., 1999.

Halliday, E. M. *Understanding Thomas Jefferson*. New York: HarperCollins, 2001.

Harris, Laurie Lanzen. *Biography For Beginners: Presidents of the United States*. Michigan: Favorable Impressions, Omnigraphics Inc., 1998.

Heilbroner, Joan. *Meet George Washington*. New York: Step-Up Books, Random House, 1989.

Joseph, Paul. *John Quincy Adams*. Minnesota: ABDO Publishing Company, 1970.

Lomask, Milton. *John Quincy Adams*. New York: Arriel Books, 1966.

Marrin, Albert. *Abraham Lincoln*. New York: Button Children's Books, 1997.

Meltzer, Milton. *The American Revolution*. New York: Thomas J. Crowell Junior Books, 1987.

Padover, Saul K. *Jefferson*. New York: Penguin Group, 1970.

Severance, John B. *Thomas Jefferson*. New York: Clarion Books, 1998.

Stern, Philip Van Doren. *The Life and Writings of Abraham Lincoln*. Random House, Inc., 1940.

Strauss, Steven D. and Spencer. *The Complete Idiot's Guide to Impeachment of the President*. New York: Alpha Books, 1998.

Shepherd, Jack. *The Adams Chronicles*. Boston: Little, Brown and Company, 1975.